IMAGES
of America

AROUND
HUNTINGTON VILLAGE

This photograph is symbolic of Huntington's heritage. The view, looking east on Main Street at the corner of Spring Road, contains much historical information that may not be evident at first glance. Main Street, then called Oyster Bay Path, was the route traveled by Richard Houldbrock, Robert Williams, and Daniel Whitehead from Oyster Bay to bargain with the Matinecock Indians for the Old First Purchase in 1653. The historical marker for the first meetinghouse is on the corner of Spring Road, then called Sabbath Day Path, and Main Street. The first Thimble Factory was located on this intersection too. Just west of this area is the Huntington Historical Society, first established in 1903. East of this point, at the summit of the hill, is the Old First Presbyterian Church, the oldest church in Huntington. The property opposite the Old First Church was home to one of the village's first schools—an elementary school—and later Huntington High School. Today, nestled among historic landmarks and appropriately placed in the old high school is Huntington Town Hall. Continuing east past the church, the road slopes downhill to the Village Green and the original town spot where the first 11 families chose to construct their first buildings. The corner of Main Street (Oyster Bay Path continuing to Cow Harbor Path) and Park Avenue (East Path) was the site of the Platt Tavern, Huntington's first tavern. All present and past structures represent proud symbols of the community's lasting strength and dedication to excellence since its birth as a town on April 2, 1653. (Huntington Historical Society.)

ON THE COVER: This is a northward view of a 1930s parade on the corner of Main Street and New York Avenue. (Huntington Historical Society.)

IMAGES
of America

AROUND
HUNTINGTON VILLAGE

Dr. Alfred V. Sforza and
Antonia S. Mattheou

ARCADIA
PUBLISHING

Published by Arcadia Publishing
Charleston, South Carolina

Library of Congress Control Number: 2012955378

For all general information, please contact Arcadia Publishing:
Telephone 843-853-2070
Fax 843-853-0044
E-mail sales@arcadiapublishing.com
For customer service and orders:
Toll-Free 1-888-313-2665

Visit us on the Internet at www.arcadiapublishing.com

To the people who have called Huntington home
and left a legacy for all to emulate.

To those whose eagerness to help with this book encouraged us to push
forward in spite of Hurricane Sandy and snowstorms Nimo and Saturn.

A special thanks to the families and friends of the authors, whose
patience, understanding, and support made this book a reality.

CONTENTS

Acknowledgments   6

Introduction   7

1.   The Way We Were   9

2.   Early Family and Places   29

3.   Places of Worship   37

4.   Law Enforcement   53

5.   Education   69

6.   Transportation   83

7.   The Dainty and the Rich   95

8.   Famous People   107

9.   Huntington Today   119

About the Historical Society   127

ACKNOWLEDGMENTS

Many thanks go to the following organizations and individuals for their contribution and assistance in the making of this book:

Jo-Ann Raia, Huntington town clerk/records management officer, for her support, input, and dedication in preserving our town's history

Huntington Town Clerk's Archives

The Huntington Historical Society

Robert (Toby) Kissam, executive director of the Huntington Historical Society, who was there every step of the way

Karen Martin, archivist of the Huntington Historical Society, for the time she spent researching and scanning images used in the book and staying late after work—Karen's keen eye for details helped present the information in this book as accurately as possible

Northport Historical Society and its director, Heather Johnson

Greenlawn Centerport Historical Association and its director, Deanne Rathke, who went out of her way to make the association's collections available and for whom multitasking is one of many strong points

Robert Hughes, Huntington town historian, for giving assistance whenever needed

Barbara Sforza, for providing a comfortable environment to work in, making all the dinners, and proofreading the material

The Walt Whitman Birthplace Association

The Cold Spring Harbor Whaling Museum

Teresa Schwind, head of adult services at the Mary Talmage Local History Room at Huntington Public Library

Jimmy Johnson, for being instrumental in clearing the path when it came to the use of some of the copyrighted images

Retired Suffolk County police officer Craig Philip Wolff, whose encouragement and persuasive nature gave birth to this book

INTRODUCTION

We shall not cease from exploration
And the end to all our exploring
Will be to arrive where we started
And know the place for the first time.

—T.S. Eliot (1888–1965)

Huntington is situated on Long Island's North Shore at the western edge of Suffolk County, about 35 miles east of New York City, on what is known as the Gold Coast of Long Island. The town comprises 93 square miles, with 60 miles of coastline, and has a population of 201,000. It is bounded by Oyster Bay on the west, Smithtown on the east, Babylon on the south, and 51 miles of the Long Island Sound beaches and harbors on the north.

The town of Huntington includes the communities of Centerport, Cold Spring Harbor, Commack, Dix Hills, East Northport, Eaton's Neck, Elwood, Fort Salonga (part in Smithtown), Greenlawn, Halesite, Half Hollow Hills, Huntington Station, Huntington Village, Melville, South Huntington, and West Hills. In addition, the town includes four incorporated villages, which have certain independent governmental powers—Asharoken, incorporated in 1925; Huntington Bay, incorporated in 1924; Lloyd Harbor, incorporated in 1926; and Northport, which became the town's first incorporated village in 1896.

The first deed for land in Huntington was made in 1646 by the Indians to New Haven governor Theophilus Eaton for the tract of land called Eaton's Neck. Eaton's (Gardiner's) Neck is a peninsula on the northeast part of Huntington that projects into the Sound. In 1798, new owners John and Joanna Gardiner deeded 10 acres to the government, and a lighthouse was built at the cost of $9,500. The Coast Guard station eventually followed.

The identity of Huntington as a town began on April 2, 1653, when three men from Oyster Bay—Richard Houldbrock, Robert Williams, and Daniel Whitehead—came eastward along Oyster Bay Path, which runs through the middle of town and is better known today as Main Street. Main Street was then a marshy section, for the headwaters of Huntington Harbor were farther inland than they are today. For the price of "6 coats, 6 kettles, 6 hatchets, 6 howes, 6 shirts, 10 knives, 6 fathoms of wampum, 3 muxes, 30 needles," the three men received a tract of land from the Matinecock Indians that extended from the Sound on the north to Cold Spring Harbor on the west ("from a certaine river or creeke on the west, commonly called by the Indyans by y name of Nachaquatuck, and by the English the Cold Spring"), Northport Harbor on the east ("to the stream at the head of Northport Harbour the Indians call Opkatkowtycke"), and to what would later be known as Old Country Road on the south. The deed is known as the Old First Purchase of 1653.

When the first settlers arrived, their homes were simple structures with sticks braced against a ridgepole and coverings of grass and dirt to keep out the elements. Some spots were already clear of timber growth, allowing the settlers to begin planting. After many seasons, the homes would

7

be improved, with solid roofs and glass, rather than parchment, for the windows. Glass would allow sunlight to enter the room, making it less dreary. Now, the shelters could be called "homes." Wooden buckets were used to get water from running brooks or wells. Nothing was wasted; shells were used to make spoons and drinking cups, and bayberries, beeswax, and tallow were used to make candles. Soap was made from fats and the lye of wood ashes, and herbs were dried for medicinal or cooking purposes. Industry came to the town as early as 1658, when merchants were trading with the West Indies, exporting barrel staves and importing rum.

Mills for grinding grains and sawing lumber, along with woolen mills and paper mills, were built on some of the streams, and tanneries were constructed for tanning leather. The West Neck area, in addition to its fine soil, contains extensive beds of clay from which bricks and pottery were made.

From 1665 to 1691, the lives of the Huntington residents were ruled by an elaborate system of jurisprudence known as "Duke's Laws." The Duke's Laws covered all aspects of life, property, mariage, Indians, churches, and taverns. It may be concluded that while many of the Duke's Laws were good, others were horrible. The laws were no model for framing our constitution; to their credit, our founding fathers looked upon some of the laws as good examples of what to avoid.

Taverns were established, selling liquor on a carefully restricted basis. Taverns and inns also served as social gathering places and convenient stops for travelers. According to the Duke's Laws, every town had to appoint an inhabitant to keep an ordinary. Thus, in 1660, Thomas Brush was appointed to keep an ordinary in Huntington. James Chichester was chosen innkeeper two years later. The Chichester house was known as the Pease and Plenty Inn. Obadiah Platt's tavern stood at the east corner of Park Avenue. George Washington dined there in April 1790, during his tour of Long Island. Mother Chidd or Chichester owned another house of entertainment at East Neck, and British and Tories were regulars there during the Revolution. This is the place Nathan Hale was seen last before being arrested by the British on September 21, 1776. The barter system was common, for very little money circulated in those early years. Gradually, different trades and businesses were established, schools were built, and the town began to expand with more buildings and more people. It may surprise many people how many hotels existed in Huntington. Grand hotels, summer resorts, and palatial homes on the bluffs, the shoreline, and the mainland provided a home and playground for the rich and famous.

The town received its charter in 1666 from Gov. Richard Nichols, who was acting on behalf of James, Duke of York (later King James II of England). The charter covered the area from Cold Spring Harbor to Nissequoque River and from Long Island Sound to the Great South Bay. The persons named in this charter were Jonas Wood, William Leveridge, Robert Seely, John Ketcham, Thomas Skidmore, Isaac Platt, Thomas Jones, and Thomas Wicks. At a special town meeting on January 27, 1872, it was voted that, as the north and south sections of the town of Huntington had "different public interests," a new town should be established. Thus, the town of Babylon was formed.

The original occupants of our town are gone. Most of the homes they occupied have also disappeared. Generations have gone by, and their struggle for existence is now only a memory, so far remote from the hardships of today. What remains are Huntington Harbor, with the everlasting hills surrounding it and the lighthouse guarding its entrance; Main Streets, museums, historical societies, libraries, theaters, shops, and restaurants bursting with life. Through these old photographs, we will do a service to our history by preserving the past and giving meaning to the life events of the people who lived here.

Come and join us for a visit of old Huntington. Perhaps together we will begin to know our hometown of Huntington "for the first time."

—Dr. Alfred V. Sforza and Antonia S. Mattheou

One

THE WAY WE WERE

The painting on the wall in Chase Bank on Main Street was originally in the Huntington Hotel. It is artist H. Willard Ortlip's concept of Chief Raseokan of the Matinecock Indians witnessing the arrival of the first settlers and attempting to explain to his warriors the meaning of the ship appearing on the horizon. Neither Indians nor settlers could foresee the changes that would transform their territory into the busy Huntington of today. (Sforza collection/Chase Bank.)

In 1653, Richard Houldbrock, Robert Williams, and Daniel Whitehead negotiated with the Matinecock Indians for the land that formed the basis of present-day Huntington. The same day, they assigned all their interests in the premises to certain residents of Huntington who became the proprietors. The items the Indians received in return for the rights to their land included six coats, six kettles, six hatchets, six hoes, six shirts, ten knives, six fathoms of wampum, thirty muxes, and thirty needles. (Town Clerk's Archives.)

This 1710 map drawn by Silas Wood shows the Nissequoque River (spelled *Niceaquage* and *Niceaquag*) and Fresh Pond (in current-day Fort Salonga). Roads that still exist include Old Country Road and Confirmation Line Road (Town Line Road). The map also indicates the boundary of the Nicholls Patent at the eastern edge and the head of Cold Spring on the west. (Town Clerk's Archives.)

In 1665, Gov. Richard Nicholls held a convention in Hempstead in order to give town grants affirming rights to land. Huntington was the fifth English settlement established in British records, thus the fifth letter in the alphabet, E, was given as its emblem. The letters HVN surrounding the E on this seal are an abbreviation of HVNtington, with V representing the Roman numeral five. To this day, the seal is used for all town-related matters. (Town Clerk's Archives.)

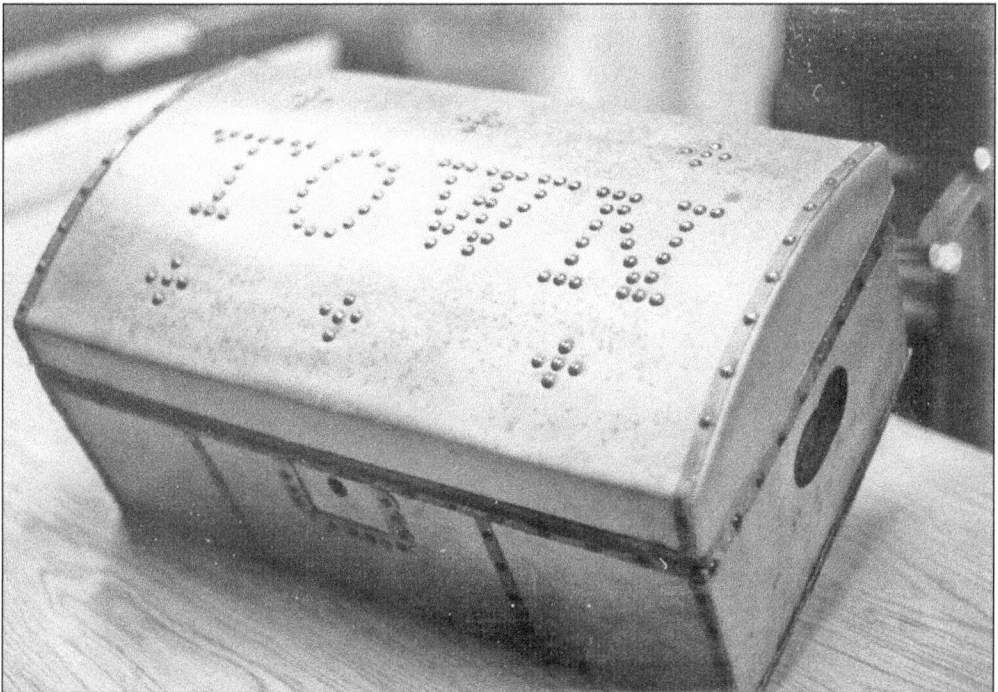

In the beginning, records were kept by the recorder (later called the town clerk) in a chest with "town" patterned with brown nails on its cover. Although inadequate in size to hold all the records, the chest was used until June 26, 1869. On that date, it was recorded that the town clerk must "procure a safe for keeping the Town papers in." Restored, this chest is still in the town's possession. (Town Clerk's Archives.)

The whaling industry flourished in Long Island from about 1820 to 1860, until the demand for oil for illumination switched to oil taken from the ground. The whaling industry made Cold Spring Harbor a scene of business activity. The *Tuscarora*, pictured here, was one of nine ships of the Cold Spring Harbor Whaling Company formed by the Jones Family. The ships had a capacity of about 2,500 barrels each. (Cold Spring Harbor Whaling Museum.)

The old paper mill stood on the northeast part of Spring Lake in Centerport. Known as the Lewis Paper Mill, it burned to the ground in 1846 and was rebuilt in 1850. In 1881, it was converted to grind grain. It was replaced in the 1930s by the Water Mill Inn and later on by Tung Ting Restaurant and the Chalet Motel. (Centerport Greenlawn Historical Association.)

William Leverich, who was also the town's first pastor, built the first mill in Huntington on Mill Street (today Mill Dam Road). It is unknown when the mill was built, but reference is made of it in 1659, when work on the dam had been delayed. (John Hulsen collection.)

The shellfish industry flourished in Huntington. Oysters, clams, and scallops from Huntington waters were shipped to New York City in great quantities every year. In 1796, the trustees of the town declared by an act that nonresidents would face a penalty of 40 shillings for fishing in town waters. (Town Clerk's Archives.)

Jesse Jarvis and Jesse Carll had shipyards on Woodbine Avenue. Carll's largest vessel, the *Mary A. Greenwood*, was 154 feet long by 33 feet wide and 17.8 feet deep with a 1,100-ton capacity. The schooner *Jesse Carll* was built in 1867 and used in the Mediterranean fruit trade. It was described as the handsomest craft of her class, and the fastest. (Northport Historical Society.)

Shipbuilding flourished in Northport in the 1800s, and a few large vessels were built and launched. Several shipyards operated on Bayview Avenue, including those of Isaac Ketcham, Edwin Lefferts, and N.R. White. Samuel P. Hartt is another name associated with shipbuilding from 1841 to the 1880s. His son Erastus served as marine architect, drafting vessel designs and laying the keels for all vessels built by the Hartt family. (Northport Historical Society.)

At the corner of Main and Spring Streets stood the Ezra Prime thimble factory, one of the major industries on Long Island in the early and mid-1800s. The thimble factory, established in 1836, was described as one of the largest in the country. Prime operated it for 40 years and died at the age of 88. The building was acquired and moved to the Old Bethpage Village Restoration. (Huntington Historical Society.)

Huntington was among the first locations in the country to manufacture silver and gold thimbles. The Primes were connected with this work for years, using the power from Meeting House Brook to turn the wheels. Ezra Prime, great-grandson of Rev. Ebenezer Prime (the third minister of the Old First Church), was the oldest thimble manufacturer in the United States. The mill was steam powered. (Huntington Historical Society.)

The Long Island Brickworks opened in 1865 at Makamah Beach. Provost Brothers also had a similar plant at Fresh Pond Road. The major consumers for the bricks were New York City builders. Brown Brothers took over the Provost Brothers plant, and their bricks, marked *BBB* (Brown's Best Bricks), are still found. Today, most of the area is occupied by the Indian Head Golf Club, and the Brown family home has served as the clubhouse since 1963. (Huntington Historical Society.)

Many streets got their names from the early industries located there. Tanyard Lane has kept its old name. A tanner built his home and business near springs and streams that were necessary in the process of tanning hides. The Cold Spring Tannery was the sole manufactory of drumheads in the United States. (Huntington Historical Society.)

Brown Brothers' Pottery,

HUNTINGTON, N. Y.

Price List of Flower Pots for 1887.

2½ inch, per hundred								$ 1.00
3 " " "								1 25
4 " " "								2 30
5 " " "								3.50
6 " " "								5.80
8 " " "								8 00
9 " " "								11.00
10 " " "								20.00
12 " " "								30.00

This price list is from the Brown Brothers Pottery. The commercial pottery industry developed on the east side of Huntington Harbor in the early 18th century and continued to manufacture both earthenware and stoneware into the 20th century. They supplied many of the Gold Coast estates with large garden pots. (Huntington Historical Society.)

The high-quality sand and clay found by Huntington Harbor was used to make bricks. It also provided the material for the Brown Brothers Pottery, which created many opportunities for African Americans and immigrants. The plant operated in Halesite near Huntington Harbor from 1863 to 1905, and their jars still adorn many houses. (Huntington Historical Society.)

Alexander Gardiner, "Greenlawn's Pickle Pioneer," was the owner of the largest farm in Greenlawn. He introduced methods of successfully growing cucumbers and cabbages and encouraged local farmers to follow his example. Cabbages were harvested in September and October and brought to the processing plants where they were cored, sliced, salted, and brined for the making of sauerkraut, a business that lasted until the 1940s. (Greenlawn Centerport Historical Association.)

Samuel Bolton was born into slavery in Virginia on January 1, 1838. Bolton came to Greenlawn in 1873. His first job was as a farmer, and he was later employed as a shareholder for Alexander Gardiner. He was nicknamed "Greenlawn's Pickle King" after growing and processing 1.5 million pickles in one season. (Greenlawn Centerport Historical Association.)

Located on Park Avenue, Obadiah Platt's Tavern at the Sign of the Half Moon and Heart was the first tavern built in the town. After Platt's death, his wife, Mary, ran the inn, which became known as "The Widow Platt's." Afterwards, it was known by their son's name, becoming the Gilbert Platt Tavern. George Washington dined here during his tour of Long Island from April 20 to April 24, 1790. (Sforza collection.)

The old Chichester House in West Hills, known as the Peace and Plenty Inn, was a stopover for stagecoaches to and from the city. Some early town meetings were held here. James Chichester was chosen as innkeeper and was reelected for many years afterward. The building is now a private residence. (Sforza collection.)

Main Street and Fire House, Huntington, L. I.

The first organized fire protection came to town in 1852. By the 1920s, the hand- and horse-drawn fire wagons of the earlier years began to give way to the new motorized fire trucks. With the advent of mechanized fire trucks, firemen would soon be able to carry their own water to the scene of a blaze. (Huntington Historical Society.)

Tuttle's Pharmacy stood on the north side of Main Street between New York and Stewart Avenues. (Huntington Historical Society.)

20

On the north side of Main Street, the O.S. Sammis Building occupied the west corner of Empire Block. Note the fire bell above George Conklin's feed store, behind which the first fire engine was housed. (Huntington Historical Society.)

The Brush Building on the south side of Main Street and New York Avenue is pictured after it was rebuilt following the disastrous fire of 1888. Note the streetlamps and the trolley. (Huntington Historical Society.)

BANK OF HUNTINGTON

Seen here in 1935, the Bank of Huntington, located on Main Street on the southeast side of New York Avenue, is presently occupied by Bank of America. James M. Brush, Henry S. Brush, and Douglas Conklin established Huntington's first bank, the Bank of James M. Brush and Company, later called the Bank of Huntington, in November 1885 with capital of $30,000. (American Photograph Company 1909.)

The original Huntington Station Bank, established on August 6, 1920, was located in the Pettit Building on the west side of New York Avenue. Later, the bank moved diagonally across the street to the corner of Broadway and New York Avenue. The bank and other buildings were demolished by urban renewal in the 1960s. (Huntington Historical Society.)

During the early days of the town's history, before superstores were invented, food stores and shops providing all kinds of services were seen on Main Street. Seen here on the north side of Main Street between New York and Stewart Avenues are M.W. Seaman Meat Market, Cohen's Clothing store, and W. Brahm's Harness shop. To this day, the intersection of New York Avenue and Main Street remains the center of the town. (Huntington Historical Society.)

Brahm's Harness Shop was on the north side of Main Street, across from Central Presbyterian Church. A dummy horse stood outside modeling feedbags, fly nets, and little hats with holes for the ears to pass through. In the winter, the horse modeled blankets and harnesses. A few blocks away, Tillotson's Harness Shop was on the south side of Main Street, west of New Street. (Huntington Historical Society.)

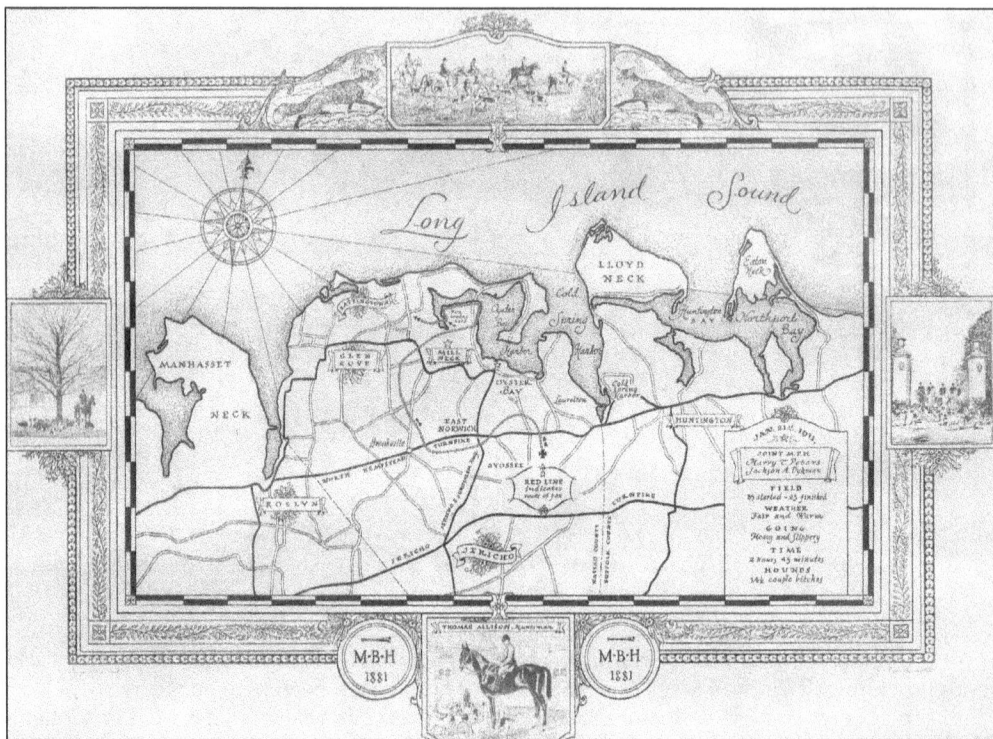

In a typical foxhunt, dogs track the fox, and the people follow on horses until someone catches and shoots the fox. The first recorded foxhunt was in Norfolk, England, in 1534. Foxhunting posses were formed regularly by rural farmers to help rid each other's lands of the foxes that posed a danger to their livestock. This map shows the route of a foxhunt on January 21, 1933. (Town Clerk's Archives.)

The Annual Highhold Games were created to show appreciation to neighbors for allowing hunters to ride through their land. They were first held on Thanksgiving Day and were later changed to Columbus Day. A notice in the *Long Islander* invited all neighbors to participate, and the event consisted of field sports and different games every year and for all ages. The Nathan Hale Band from Huntington High School was invited. (Huntington Historical Society.)

24

The Opera House stood on the north side of Main Street near the corner of Stewart Avenue. Built in 1892, it was a scene of musical, literary, and civic events. The Opera House was destroyed by fire on March 15, 1910. (Huntington Historical Society.)

The Opera House also hosted many events, such as a poultry exhibit on January 21 and 22, 1910. (Huntington Historical Society.)

The talent show or "parada" was a popular event during wintertime. The performers were local people who tried out for the parts, and they often improvised their own acts and familiar songs. The show featured solos, beautifully costumed choruses, soft-shoe numbers, and a minstrel performance. Local comedians Sam Cheshire and Kate Williams always performed. (Huntington Historical Society.)

In 1656, Native Americans signed a deed giving settlers the rights to the land known as Cow Harbor, or Opcatkontycke, which means "wading place creek." Today, this area is the incorporated village of Northport. This is a westward view of Main Street from around 1905. On the left is St. Paul's Methodist Church. The house next to it was demolished to enlarge the church's manse. (Northport Historical Society.)

The Winter Carnival was a major yearly event in Huntington. It included bobsledding, horse-drawn sleigh races, and a hog weight guessing contest. The last races were held in 1920. That year, a racing accident involving the all-women Greyhound bobsled team occurred. The team lost control of their sled and collided with a tree, and most of the women sustained serious injuries. The races continued for that day, but never again. (Huntington Historical Society.)

The date for the Winter Carnival events was determined by the weather. Races started at the top of Lawrence Hill Road, traveled down through Main Street, and ended on the hill by the old town hall. Sometimes, they would go as far as Spring Road. Huntington teams as well as those from other villages on Long Island entered the races. (Huntington Historical Society.)

In the late 1800s, the property about one mile south of the railroad tracks and east of Depot Road (then called Fairground Avenue) was converted into a fairground with a one-mile horse-racing track. The racetrack was not a big success. The name *Fairground* outlasted it, as it was the original name of the hamlet, later changed to Huntington Station. Today, private homes cover the racetrack area. (Huntington Historical Society.)

A.S. Pettit was the first railroad agent and became the first postmaster. The first post office was established July 24, 1890, with the designation of Fairground, Long Island. In 1898, Pettit moved the post office to his new place of business near the railroad station, on the west side of New York Avenue. On August 12, 1912, the name of the post office was changed from Fairground to Huntington Station. (Huntington Historical Society.)

Two

EARLY FAMILY AND PLACES

Latting's Hundred is located at 424 Park Avenue in Huntington. It has been occupied continuously since 1653 and served as a working farm for 300 years. Early town offices, a general store, an inn, a post office, and a newspaper were also housed here. It was used for military purposes during the Revolution and the War of 1812. African American residents manumitted under state law received their freedom papers here. (Rex Metcalf collection.)

This is the Conklin House before it was restored to its original condition. The building is situated on New York Avenue and High Street. The Conklin Homestead was deeded to the Huntington Historical Society in 1911 by Ella J. Conklin Hurd. The oldest part is the low wing on the right of the entrance. (Huntington Historical Society.)

The Kissam House, one of the original home lots that faced the old Town Green, was built in 1795 by Timothy Jarvis. It was first occupied by Dr. Daniel Whitehead Kissam, a physician from Oyster Bay. Considered one of the most outstanding three-quarter plan houses on Long Island, it is noted for its fine architectural details. (Huntington Historical Society.)

In 1711, Henry and Rebecca Lloyd inherited a 3,000-acre parcel of land in Lloyd Neck that had been owned by Henry's father, James Lloyd I. Henry built a four-room manor home in the post-medieval architectural style. Today, it is one of the few surviving examples of this style of architecture. When Henry died in 1763, he left the manor to his four sons. He also left money to his slave Jupiter Hammon, the first published African American poet in the colonies. (Huntington Historical Society.)

Henry Lloyd began clearing the land for his flocks of sheep, orchards, barns, blacksmith's shop, school, cemetery, and farms. He also rented land to tenant farmers, from whom he collected annual quitrents. His apple-cider trading business in the English colonies and the Caribbean earned the family a considerable amount of money. (Huntington Historical Society.)

Erected in 1891 and designed by Henry Bacon—famous for his Lincoln Memorial—the Soldiers & Sailors Museum is a memorial to the dead of the Civil War. Rufus Prime, father of Cornelia and Temple Prime, headed the committee that arranged for its construction. It later served as the town's first library and became part of the Union Free School District in 1929. (American Photograph Company, 1909.)

In 1914, Andrew Carnegie donated $10,000 toward a structure to house the Northport Library. This building on Main Street and Woodbine Avenue has served as Northport's public library, has been used to support efforts during World Wars I and II, and has functioned as a workplace during the Depression where women would mend donated clothes for needy families. (Northport Historical Society.)

The old town hall on Main Street, built by the prestigious New York architectural firm of Peabody, Wilson & Brown, served Huntington starting in 1911. The Neoclassical facade of the building features a monumental front with a portico, marble trim, colossal Corinthian columns, a cornice, and a clock tower. (Huntington Historical Society.)

The Arsenal stood on the south tip of the Town Green next to the Poor House. The first recorded sale was to blacksmith Samuel Jarvis, who plied his trade here in 1800. (Huntington Historical Society.)

In 1835, Thomas Brush purchased a 140-acre farm with the house north of Old Field Road. Clara Knap bought the farm in 1910 and added barns, outbuildings, and a water-storage tower. When Doctor Carpenter bought the farm, he added a west wing in the 1930s and an east wing in 1950. The property was eventually acquired by the town of Huntington and is being maintained as a farm; the structures have been demolished. (Greenlawn Centerport Historical Association.)

Walt Whitman founded the *Long Islander* newspaper in 1838. It was printed with handset type on a hand press in the loft of a barn off Main Street and Whitman hand delivered all his newspapers. The paper's location on the northwest corner of Main Street and Clinton Street was erected in 1889. This publication is still in circulation. (Huntington Historical Society.)

The Smith-Gardiner farmhouse on Park Avenue was built by Henry Smith around 1752. Henry's son Alexander and daughter-in-law were murdered here in 1842 by farm helper Antoine Keisler. Henry's great-grandson Alexander Gardiner, who grew up in this house, remodeled and enlarged it in the 1860s. Alexander's granddaughter Alice and her twin brothers Herbert and Harold were born in the farmhouse and lived here all their lives. (Greenlawn Centerport Historical Association.)

On Centershore Road and Route 25A stands the Suydam Homestead, which was built around 1730. Originally, this was a one-room structure. More rooms and a kitchen were added later, and the roof was raised to accommodate a bedroom. From the early 1800s to the 1950s, the house was owned by the Suydam family. (Greenlawn Centerport Historical Association.)

Built before 1816 by Walt Whitman Sr. (a descendant of Joseph Whitman, who settled in Huntington in the 1660s), this house is situated on Walt Whitman Road, a mile south of Jericho Turnpike. On May 31, 1952, it was dedicated as a shrine to the spirit of democracy. (Walt Whitman Birthplace Association.)

In 1698, the town trustees divided a large tract of land in the southwest part of the town among a large number of individuals. John Buffet was one of them. John married Hannah Titus, daughter of Samuel Titus, another individual who was granted land in the same area. Warren Buffet and his sister Doris are descendants of John. (Town clerk archives.)

Three

PLACES OF WORSHIP

The Old First Presbyterian Church, built in 1658, is the oldest church in Huntington. This large, white shingled structure just east of town on Main Street is a landmark. Its first minister was Rev. William Leverich (1658–1669), who was also Huntington's first miller. Initially organized as a Congregational church, from 1748 to the present, it has been Presbyterian. (Huntington Historical Society.)

During the pastorate of Rev. Samuel T. Carter (1868–1908), the 13th pastor of the Old First Church, a chapel was built in Huntington Station. A document from the church, dated May 15, 1894, described a parcel of land purchased in Fairground (Huntington Station) "for the sum of forty five dollars, lawful money of the United States" for the construction of the chapel. (Huntington Historical Society.)

The deli and Freddie's Shoe Repairs, at 1169 and 1171 New York Avenue, were built in the exact location of the chapel. This photograph was taken during the Huntington Station Urban Renewal around the 1960s. (Huntington Historical Society.)

St. John's Episcopal Church (1748) was located on Park Avenue opposite Huntington Hospital. This first church building was used until 1861. On May 6, 1862, a second church edifice was consecrated. This building was used until 1905, when it was destroyed by fire. (Huntington Historical Society.)

Many did not want to leave the beautiful wooded spot, and the selection of a building site resulted in a serious division among the parishioners. It was decided to build the new St. John's Episcopal Church on a more convenient and central location, on Prospect Street and Main Street in the village. The first service was held in the new church on Palm Sunday 1908. (Huntington Historical Society.)

In Halesite, on the Harbor Road (East Shore Road), the Meade family owned a corncrib, which they gave to the church to use as a chapel. The altar and lectern were the ones used in the first St. John's Church in 1748. The chapel was known as St. Andrews-By-The-Sea. Today, the building is a private residence. (Huntington Historical Society.)

St. John's Episcopal Church was the first to be established in Cold Spring Harbor. The first services were held in a 1790 little red schoolhouse located near the site of the present church. On September 4, 1831, the members decided to build a new church. In the beginning, the structure had no steeple, but one was added soon afterwards. (Huntington Historical Society.)

The Huntington Methodist Church was built in 1829 just east of the old *Long Islander* building. The original site was purchased for $95. Daniel Sammis was in charge of building the church, and much of the material used was cut in his sawmill. The first church was simple in design, with no steeple or other adornments. It was lighted by candles in wooden candlesticks that were turned at the mill. (Huntington Historical Society.)

As membership increased, Huntington Methodist rebuilt the original structure in 1863 and then again in 1900. The new building had a steeple with a four-sided clock, which could be seen from all directions. People depended on the clock and on the bell, which rang every hour, during their normal working-day routines. (Huntington Historical Society.)

Cold Spring Harbor Methodist Church held its first church meeting on October 17, 1842. In 1995, it merged with Huntington Methodist to form the United Methodist Church, located on West Neck Road in Huntington. In 1995, the Society for Preservation of Long Island Antiquities purchased the building. (Huntington Historical Society.)

The Ketewamoke Chapter House of the Daughters of the American Revolution on Nassau Road was also the former Universalist Church, established in 1837. (DAR Collection/Lillian Najarian.)

In 1869, the Universalists bought a lot at the northeast corner of New York Avenue and Elm Street. There, they erected a church that was dedicated on February 3, 1871. (Huntington Historical Society.)

Two stone columns south of St. Patrick's Cemetery on Huntington Road represent the entrance to the first Roman Catholic church in West Neck, built in 1849. St. Patrick's Cemetery is in the background. The church was destroyed by fire in February 1867. (Sforza Collection.)

A new church, now called St. Patrick's Church, was built on the southeast corner of Main Street and Anderson Place. The church was built at a cost of $29,000 despite the fact that, at the time, this was a poor parish. (Huntington Historical Society.)

On June 23, 1963, a new St. Patrick's Church was dedicated on Main Street between Ackerman Place and Anderson Place on the former site of the school playground. (Sforza collection.)

On April 26, 1864, a group of petitioners, mostly from the Old First Church, organized the Second Presbyterian Church on Main Street in Huntington Village. A fire on September 12, 1888, destroyed 200 feet of buildings on Main Street east of New York Avenue, including the Second Presbyterian Church. (Huntington Historical Society.)

When rebuilt, the religious institution's name was changed in 1899 to Central Presbyterian Church of Huntington. (Huntington Historical Society.)

In August 1868, members of the Cold Spring Harbor Baptist Church decided to form a church of their own in Huntington. At a meeting on September 6, 1868, Rev. Lanson Steward was selected as the first pastor. In 1870, land was purchased on Green Street, and a small church was erected and dedicated on December 8, 1870. (Huntington Historical Society.)

In 1924, the expanding membership of the Huntington Baptist Church considered building a new church. They purchased land on the present site of the church at the corner of High Street and Oakwood Road. Church member R.A. Lewis was awarded the contract to build the new structure, and work on the present church began in 1927 and was completed in January 1929. (Mattheou photograph.)

The first synagogue was built in 1911 on Church Street in Huntington Station. (Sforza Collection.)

On May 23, 1955, property was acquired on Park Avenue, which included part of the old William Teich farm, and the new Huntington Jewish Center became a reality. On April 21, 1961, the first Friday-night services were celebrated in the new building. Said during the service was the following: "Let us also plan to work together in peace and harmony, ever striving to make our new home symbolic of love and faith and hope . . . today's dedication to tomorrow." (Sforza collection.)

In 1908, St. Peter's Lutheran Church was founded. In the beginning, services were held in the Old First Presbyterian Chapel in Huntington Station. In 1912, a new church was built on the corner of Fairground Avenue and Second Street in Huntington Station. Paul H. Pallmeyer became the new pastor. In 1956, the church was purchased by the Suffolk Hellenic Community to serve Greek Orthodox families in Huntington. (Pallmeyer Collection.)

After purchasing St. Peter's Lutheran Church, St. Paraskevi parishioners worshiped there until disaster struck in December 1963. The heating system exploded during the night, and the church burned to the ground. Land was purchased on Shrine Place and Pulaski Road in Greenlawn, and a new church was constructed and dedicated on July 25, 1966, the feast day of patron saint Paraskevi. (Mattheou photograph.)

An old exhibition building on the fairgrounds at Huntington Station, seating about 1,000 people, was purchased and remodeled as an auxiliary chapel to St. Patrick's Church. The chapel was named St. Hugh's, and in 1913, it became an independent parish. (Huntington Historical Society.)

A new church was added to the St. Hugh of Lincoln chapel and dedicated in 1953. On September 28, 1986, a fire severely damaged the building, and the restored church was opened on April 18, 1987. (Huntington Historical Society.)

In 1953, Our Lady Queen of Martyrs began as a mission for St. Philip Neri Church in a restored boathouse on the property of Regina Brunswick. The boathouse was transformed into a chapel and received parish status in 1966. (Our Lady Queen of Martyrs Archives.)

In 1982, Our Lady Queen of Martyrs parish decided to build a new church instead of restoring the old boat garage. The new building was erected within two years and was dedicated on September 23, 1984. (Sforza collection.)

In 1919, a few Christian Scientists in Huntington met at a private home and held a service. By 1957, a new church was built on the corner of Main and Woolsey Streets, and was dedicated on September 24, 1961. (Sforza collection.)

The early black community of Huntington organized the Bethel African Methodist Episcopal (AME) Church in 1843 on the former site of St. John's Episcopal Church, opposite Huntington Hospital. (Mattheou photograph.)

The Grotto-Shrine at St. Paraskevi Greek Orthodox Church was erected in 1969 with funding provided by the family of John Iakovou. The grotto is an exact replica of the original shrine at Therapia, Turkey. It is believed that the water of the spring at Therapia has miraculous healing powers for vision disorders. The plaque over the Grotto's entrance is dedicated to Iakovou's mother: "To my mother Anastasia, who taught me to see." (Mattheou photograph.)

The Commack United Methodist Church on Townline Road was erected in 1789 and is the oldest Methodist church in the state of New York. In 1968, the Methodist Church and the Evangelical United Brethren merged and built a larger sanctuary on the premises. The facilities are also used by the Korean United Methodist Church, which provides a program for Korean-speaking families. (Mattheou photograph.)

Four

LAW ENFORCEMENT

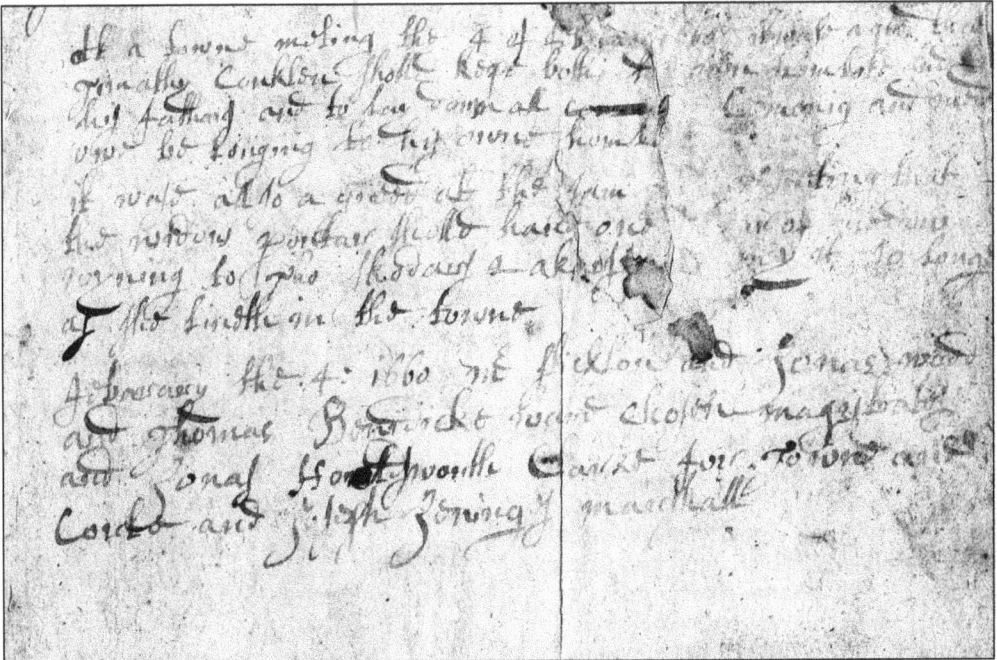

According to Huntington town records from February 4, 1660, Jonas Holdsworth was the first to be referred to as "clarke for the Town and Corte" (a position previously known as recorder). Joseph Jeninges (Jennings) was selected as the town's first marshal. (Town Clerk's Archives.)

Huntington town records from April 6, 1663, document John Lome's selection as the first constable. (Town Clerk's Archives.)

Huntington constables Moses White and Alexander Sammis are pictured in the late 1800s. Some say that the word *cop*, a slang word for "policeman," may have come from the abbreviation COP, which stood for "constable on patrol." At first, rural communities had little need for a full-time police officer. In the beginning, the responsibility of providing police protection was with individual towns and villages, and town officials appointed a constable. (Sforza collection.)

In 1880, Sarah and Robert Williams sold a parcel of land for $125 to the town of Huntington to be used as a town lockup. (Town Clerk's Archives.)

The town lockup was located on the west side of New York Avenue, north of 25A near Gibson Avenue (near the location of the present Burger King). (Huntington Historical Society.)

In 1913, John Trainer was appointed as Huntington's first regular police officer. For $30, he was expected not only to be the police officer, but also janitor, custodian, and jack-of-all-trades for the town. Trainer directed traffic from the police traffic booth in the middle of the intersection of New York Avenue and Main Street. (Sforza collection.)

The police traffic booth is pictured here in the early 1900s. Mounted on top of the booth was a stop-and-go sign, which the police officer inside could turn by hand in the proper direction. If for any reason the booth was unoccupied, the officer would put the sign at a 45-degree angle to signify caution. The booth protected the officer from careless drivers as well as from the wind, rain, and snow. (Huntington Historical Society.)

Town records from January 1933 document the formation of the Huntington Police Department. (Sforza photograph/Town Clerk's Archives.)

Huntington Police Department
January 1st 1933

Huntington Town Records

Town Meeting January 4, 1933

The matter of the police organization as passed on October 11th was acted upon as follows

WHEREAS, by resolution, as of October 11th, 1932, this Town Board voted to establish a police force to effective

On and after January 1, 1933, now therefore it be

RESOLVED:

That **John Trainer, Clarence Phillips, Leo Cass, James Miller, Edward Juliano and William Slattery**

are police officers of the Town of

Huntington, to be paid $175 per month, and that only as

compensation for their services as said police officers.

CARRIED.

This is the Huntington Police Department in April 1933. Pictured are, from left to right, (top row) John Trainer, Clarence Phillips, James Miller, Gus Henneborn, and Irving Wiggins; (middle row) Edward Juliano, Ray Leighton, and Chief Leo Cass; (bottom row) William Slattery, William Van Size, Archie Brooks, and Albert Ager. (Sforza collection.)

Controversy followed John Hulsen from his position as constable in the early 1900s, to deputy sheriff, motorcycle police, and sergeant in the Huntington Police Department to his role as town Republican leader in the 1950s. Many who knew John personally still debate the conflicts that occurred in this man's career, but none will disagree about his ability as a police officer and the brave acts he performed in the line of duty. (Huntington Historical Society.)

Known to his friends as "Bill," Charles William Brown began his career in the Huntington Police Department in 1947. Police work was not his only expertise. Also known as "Gorilla Bill" for his boxing ability, he was named Newsday Golden Gloves Champion. When the Huntington Police Department merged and became part of the Suffolk County Police Department, Bill became the first commander of the second precinct in Huntington. (Sforza collection.)

The Huntington Police Department is shown here in front of old town hall in the 1950s. Pictured are, from left to right, (first row) Sgt. Ray Leighton, Sgt. Frank Brown, Sgt. John Yacino, Huntington town supervisor Walter Fasbender, Chief Clarence Phillips, and Sgt. William Byrnes; (second row) Thomas Burns, James Miller, James C. Ronaghan, William Blunt, Charles Brown, and Hewlett Johnson; (third row) Julian Holcombe, Gus Dobler, Paul Arato, Edward Donahue, Anthony Aurricchio, and James Indiere; (fourth row) John Coppins, Victor Gardella, Stanley Winter, John Robertson, Stephen Maciura, and Jack Impellizzeri; (fifth row) Eugene Hamilton, James P. Ronaghan, Wilbur Morrell, Regis O'Neil, William Weyaurgh, Joseph DeRiso, and John Hoffman; (sixth row) Richard Robertson, Edward Hehir, Joseph York, Edward Woiczeckowski, Carl Keuhne, and Jeremiah Mills; (seventh row) Hugo Romler, William Schouw, Edward Richard, and Salvatore Caracci. (Sforza collection.)

The Huntington Police Department Motorcycle Division is seen in front of the police department garage on Gerard Street. The men are, from left to right, Charlie Winter, Frank Dobson, Billy Blunt, Hewlett "Buddy" Johnson, Harold Lewis, and Eugene LaPeter. (Sforza collection.)

This image shows Ed Richard of the motorcycle division and Jim Indiere questioning a lost child. Police at the time had no cell phones and had to make sure they kept a supply of "one thin dime" to phone in and connect with the police desk officer. They also had to know where all the public telephones were just in case they needed help. (Sforza collection.)

These members of the motorcycle division are seen on parade duty on New York Avenue just south of Main Street. In 1958, their annual salary was $4,300. There was no overtime allowed. All court time, parade duty, hearings, and trials were mandatory and without compensation. They also had to buy their own uniforms and pay for their own health insurance and retirement. (Sforza collection.)

Ed Richard of the motorcycle division comforts a young boy after a hit-and-run accident. The boy asked Ed "am I going to die?" Ed assured him he would be well, but the boy died on the way to the hospital. The young man with the glasses and dark hair at right rear is Arthur Hadel, who in 1959 would be in the last class to join the Huntington Police Department. (Sforza collection.)

At one time the Huntington Police Department acquired two bloodhounds. "The use of these blood hounds did not last too long," Sgt. Ed Richard said. "We had no reason to use them and it cost too much to take care of them and feed them." Sergeant Richard is shown with Patches the bloodhound at left and below, in front of the Huntington Police Department precinct on Main Street in Huntington Village. (Both, Sforza collection.)

Three Huntington Police Department Marine Division boats are seen here leaving Huntington Harbor. (Sforza collection.)

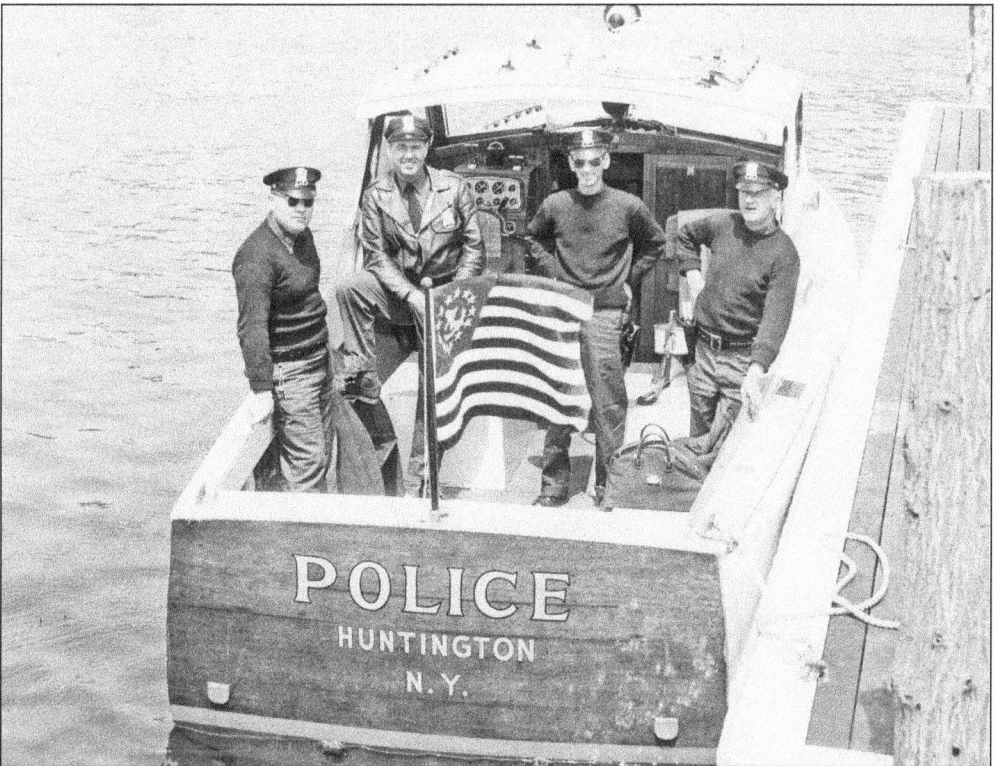

The Huntington Police Marine Division included Jack McCrickert, Ed Richard, Paul Arato, and Voyle "Andy" Anderson. (Sforza collection.)

On January 1, 1960, the Huntington Police Department merged with other Suffolk County departments to form the Suffolk County Police Department. Two police boats, *Marine Alpha* and *Marine Bravo*, were assigned to Huntington Harbor. *Marine Alpha* is shown here dragging the water for a drowning victim. (Sforza collection.)

Ed Richard, with his expertise gained during his war years with the Coast Guard, helped Chief Alfred Kohler form the new marine division of the Huntington Police Department. The ever-expanding department now increased its protection of both land and water. (Sforza collection.)

Pictured here, the Huntington Police Department graduating class of 1959 was the last group to be called the Huntington Police Department before merging and forming the Suffolk County Police on January 1, 1960. (Sforza collection.)

The Huntington Police Department patch (upper left) had gold lettering on a field of blue. After the merger with the Suffolk County Police Department, the patch underwent three transformations. The first (upper right) had gold lettering on a blue field; the second (bottom left) was the same patch with "N.Y." added; the third, present-day patch (bottom right) features gold lettering on a field of red. (Sforza collection Portrait of a Small Town II/ patches courtesy of Arthur Hadel.)

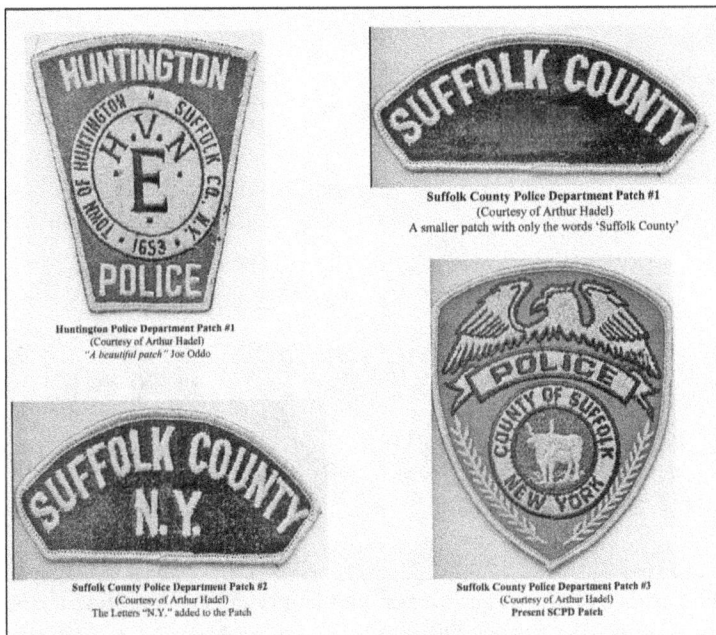

Huntington Police Department Patch #1
(Courtesy of Arthur Hadel)
"A beautiful patch" Joe Oddo

Suffolk County Police Department Patch #1
(Courtesy of Arthur Hadel)
A smaller patch with only the words 'Suffolk County'

Suffolk County Police Department Patch #2
(Courtesy of Arthur Hadel)
The Letters "N.Y." added to the Patch

Suffolk County Police Department Patch #3
(Courtesy of Arthur Hadel)
Present SCPD Patch

On January 1, 1960, the former home of the Huntington Police Department on Main Street became the home of the Suffolk County Police Department 2nd Precinct (Sforza collection.)

This is the new home of the Suffolk County Police Department 2nd Precinct on Park Avenue in Huntington. (Sforza collection.)

This photograph was taken on Sunday, December 30, 1962. The year 1962 ended with a cold blast. Freezing temperatures as low as six degrees below zero and winds up to 75 miles per hour were recorded in Huntington. The weather hindered the town's firemen and police, and the ice in Huntington Bay made navigating the waters hazardous and would have hindered any rescue efforts that were needed. (Sforza collection.)

In December of 1962, a tugboat named the *Gwendoline Steers* sank and disappeared on a trip from New York to Northport. Bodies of the frozen crew members started to surface the first day after the boat suddenly vanished and continued for many months until the last body surfaced in May. (Steve Knox and the *Gwendoline Steers* memorial website.)

On December 31, 1962, at 7:00 a.m., the Coast Guard and marine police discovered a single, ice-covered lifeboat washed ashore. It contained a shredded life preserver and the body of one person wedged under the front seat with his left wrist lashed to the side of the boat. The body, encased in a block of ice, was later identified as that of Hugh A. Reid of Brooklyn, an engineer on the *Gwendoline Steers*. (Sforza collection.)

On January 5, 1963, divers and special ships equipped with sonar were still unable to locate the *Gwendoline Steers*. Meanwhile, two more bodies floated ashore. Capt. Herbert Dickman washed up at Nissequoque Town Beach, while deckhand Robert E. Knox was discovered at West Meadow Beach in Stony Brook (Sforza collection.)

Five

EDUCATION

The Huntington Academy was one of the four 18th-century academic institutions on Long Island. Organized and financed by a group of 50 public-spirited citizens, the building was erected in 1793 on the hill near the center of the village. It was "two stories in height, forty feet in length and twenty-four feet wide" with a belfry. The curriculum was liberal and varied, and many students attended the school in preparation for college. (Huntington Historical Society.)

The first schoolmaster was Jonas Holdsworth, who probably sailed from England to Virginia in 1635. He moved to Huntington in 1657 and was hired as a teacher. In 1661, he became town clerk. The details described in his teaching contract lead to the conclusion that the undertaking was considered most important by the residents of Huntington. (Town Clerk's Archives.)

The Huntington Union Free School was established on April 13, 1857, the first in New York state. George A. Scudder, Brewster Conklin, Brewster Skidmore, Richard B. Post, George Woodhull, and Smith Conklin constituted the first board of education. A three-story wood school was built in 1858 at the site of the old academy for a cost of $6,000. In 1909, it was razed and replaced by the Huntington High School. (Huntington Historical Society.)

The Main Street Elementary School was built in 1898 at the cost of $5,000 to accommodate kindergarten through eighth-grade youngsters. The brick building served as a grammar school until the Village Green School was constructed in 1952, at which time it became the annex to Huntington (R.L. Simpson) High School. The building is now part of the Huntington Town Hall. (Huntington Historical Society.)

Huntington High School, built in 1909 at the cost of $105,000, featured accommodations and equipment for laboratory work, manual training and trade school work, drawing, and other necessary departments of a modern curriculum. It had a gymnasium, a library, a botany room, three floors of classrooms, and offices. In 1950, it was renamed R.L. Simpson High School in honor of Robert L. Simpson, principal of Huntington High School from 1930 to 1950. (Huntington Historical Society.)

When the School Street School was built in Huntington Station in 1906, there were not enough children to fill the whole building. As only two rooms were needed, the shutters were closed on half of the building. The bell on top of the building came from the Union School building on Main Street. It was kept in storage and rediscovered years later by custodian Bill Falcone, and is now on display in Huntington High School. (Huntington Historical Society.)

The population of Huntington Station had been growing, and the Lowndes Avenue School was built in 1913 at the cost of $58,000 to serve as a school for kindergarten through eighth grade. Although it was larger than the School Street School, an addition had to be built in 1926, doubling its size. (Huntington Historical Society.)

Upon completion of the addition, the Lowndes Avenue School was renamed Roosevelt Elementary School in honor of Theodore Roosevelt. Demolished in the 1970s, it was replaced by the Jack Abrams Intermediate School. (Huntington Historical Society.)

This is the 1947 second-grade class of Roosevelt Elementary School. Pictured are, from left to right, (first row) Ron Hellman, unidentified, Carl Mattarrazzo, Dan Istvan, John LoScalzo, Harold Roberts, and John "Biffy" Garafolo; (second row) Wilma Lundstrom, Anita Piper, Ken Skidmore, Sheldon Shalant, Bill Torrans, Al Sforza, unidentified, and Pat Ordway; (third row) Ronald Sposato, Don Hellman, Beatrice Karpis, Dave Weinstein, Mrs. Ormand, Wayne Zoll, unidentified, Karl Wolter, and John Benjamin. (Sforza Collection.)

The Woodbury Avenue Elementary School, completed in 1924, held students from Kindergarten through eighth grade. When R.K. Toaz Jr. High School opened in 1939, Woodbury Avenue School and the other elementary schools in town were reorganized to serve only students in kindergarten through sixth grade. Closed in 1971, it was rented to the Board of Cooperative Educational Services (BOCES) and later to a Christian school. The building and land were sold, demolished, and replaced by condominium units. (Huntington Historical Society.)

As the population of Huntington Station once again steadily increased, a new school named Lincoln School opened in September 1925 on Ninth Street in Huntington Station. It originally served students in kindergarten through eighth grade. Closed in the early 1970s, it served as a school for students with special educational needs. The building was eventually sold and converted to a 30-apartment complex. (Huntington Historical Society.)

This is the Lincoln School Dramatic Club in 1931. Pictured are, from left to right, (first row) Eugene Edstron and Martin Hassett; (second row) Anna Smith, Dorothy Munday, Regina Brengel, Gladys Tapley, Evelyn Williams, Minnie Sposato, and Frances Gordon; (third row) Anna Holawite, Margaret Herting, Josephine Walters, Elfrieda Busse, Catherine Olson, and Camille Guarine; (fourth row) Oscar Olson. (Jack Abrams collection.)

This photograph is of the Lincoln Elementary School sixth-grade class of 1952. Pictured are, from left to right, (first row) Helene Scola, "Binky" Holstein, Lou Fusaro, Jerry Sarentino, Alfonse Muno, Peggy ?, Robert Kerner, and George Deal; (second row) Dorothy Bateman, Emil Ortalloni, Ed Shea, Wayne Carbino, Barbara Albin, Kate Maas, John Alessio, and Dolores Scola; (third row) Malcolm Itter, MiMi MacNamara, Warren Kraus, John Florio, Carlene Honahan, Phyllis Stubbollo, Barbara Tapley, and Rich Provenzano; (fourth row) Principal Walter Reed, Rich Klein, Barbara Bukow, Ruth Warnquest, Tom Becker, Pat Anderson, Phil Ferdinando, Jeanette Henry, unidentified, and sixth-grade teacher Mrs. Monroe. (Sforza collection.)

R.K. Toaz Jr. High School opened on September 5, 1939, and was the first junior high school in Suffolk. Located on Woodhull and Nassau Roads, it was constructed by the Federal Emergency Works Project Administration. The school served seventh-, eighth-, and ninth-grade students and was named after Huntington's superintendent of schools R.K. Toaz (1906–1933). The school closed on June 25, 1982, and was sold to Touro Law School. (Huntington Historical Society.)

The Nathan Hale School on Bay Avenue has been turned into condominiums. (Huntington Historical Society.)

Pictured here is Long Swamp School at the intersection of Depot, Maplewood, and Melville Roads in Huntington Station. Prior to this building, there was a one-room wooden structure that housed eight grades. Boys sat on one side of the room, and girls on the other. (Huntington Historical Society.)

West Hills Public School on Jericho Turnpike is pictured here. (Huntington Historical Society.)

The Jericho Turnpike School has been the site of Walt Whitman High School since 1960.
(Huntington Historical Society.)

The 22-by-24-foot, one-room Greenlawn School, on Greenlawn Road near Tilden Lane in Centerport, was built on half an acre of land purchased from Luther and Celia Brush in 1872. The total cost, which included the desks, was $1,095. In 1905, there were 31 children attending school. Prior to that, the academic year was six months, and classes were held at local farmhouses. (Greenlawn Centerport Historical Association.)

Woodhull School opened in 1967 to serve students in kindergarten through sixth grade. When Roosevelt Elementary School was demolished as a result of the Huntington Station Urban Renewal projects, students from that area came to the Woodhull School. (Mattheou photograph.)

The Village Green School, located on Park Avenue just south of Main Street, opened in 1952. C. Harold Kincaid was the principal. There were 20 teachers, and the enrollment was expected to reach 550 students. It was the last elementary school built in the district. The school closed in 1973 and is the present site of the senior citizens center and the Cinema Arts Theater. (Huntington Historical Society.)

The first Cold Spring Harbor School, "Bungtown School," was built in 1790 near St. John's Church in Cold Spring Harbor. It featured a chimney and a large fireplace. The structure was demolished because of deterioration, and a new building, erected in 1896 opposite Moore's Hill Road, served the community until 1940. The present school building stands one-fifth of a mile down Laurel Hill Road. (Huntington Historical Society.)

In 1909, the Northport Public School was situated on the hill above Scudder Avenue. (American Photograph Company, 1909.)

The Trade School was built in 1906 by Cornelia Prime. Designed by Cady, Berg & See (the architects of the original Metropolitan Opera House and the American Museum of Natural History), this unusually shaped building originally housed one of America's first vocational schools. Today, it is the home of the Huntington Historical Society. (Huntington Historical Society.)

On the corner of Main Street and Woodbury Road was the home of Mrs. Ezra Conklin. In the mid-1800s, Mrs. Conklin had established a private school in her home. After the church purchased the building, it functioned as a rectory for many years. The site is now the home of St. Patrick's School, which opened on September 6, 1922. (Huntington Historical Society.)

The Ezra Prime home was built in 1867 on what is now the site of Heckscher Park. It was used as a school while the new high school was being built in 1909. (Huntington Historical Society.)

The Brickyards School was used by children of employees in the Crossman Brickyards. (Huntington Historical Society.)

Six

TRANSPORTATION

The first street transportation in Huntington was a horse-drawn stage between the harbor in Halesite and the Long Island Railroad in Huntington Station. The stage was eventually replaced by horse-drawn cars, which were built and operated by a company made up of local people. "Uncle Jesse" Conklin (1815–1895) drove the stage to and from the railroad station and carried the mail for 56 years. In all those years, he only missed one train, and that was the first time he carried a watch. He never missed a train after that incident, and he never carried the watch again. This stagecoach was his "new stage," with up-to-date accessories like glass windows and back steps. (Huntington Historical Society.)

Originally, before steamboats, all ferryboats were either rowboats or pirogues (small, light, flat-bottomed boats). Eventually, boats powered by horses on a treadmill provided faster service. At one time, horse-drawn boats competed with steamboats in the thriving business of ferrying passengers from Manhattan to Brooklyn. One such ferry, powered by eight horses, could carry more than 200 passengers across the East River in eight to eighteen minutes. (Northport Historical Society.)

Ferry service improved with the use of sailboats, which were large enough to carry cattle, horses, and carriages. The disadvantage was that crossing had to wait for winds and tides to change. As a result, people stayed in inns or hotels, waiting to cross the river. (Town Clerk's Archives.)

When ferries were built with steam engines, boats could make regular trips across the river regardless of winds and tides. Service between Huntington and Norwalk, Connecticut, was established in 1765 when the town trustees hired out the ferry to Elisha Gilbert. The ferry had to be sufficient to carry six men and six horses. The steamer *Huntington* was the first ferry to Norwalk in 1765. (Town Clerk's Archives.)

East River Bridge.
Plan of one Tower
1600 feet Span

When bridges and tunnels were built, ferries lost their importance. The Brooklyn Bridge in New York City is one of the oldest suspension bridges in the United States. Completed in 1883, it connects the boroughs of Manhattan and Brooklyn by spanning the East River. On its first day, a total of 1,800 vehicles and 150,300 people crossed what was then the only land passage between Manhattan and Brooklyn. (National Archives.)

On January 13, 1840, the steamship *Lexington*, carrying 100 passengers and a load of cotton bales, was scheduled to reach Stonington, Connecticut. The cotton caught fire as the steamship was passing Eaton's Neck, and despite rescue attempts by residents of the area, only four passengers survived. (Northport Historical Society.)

In 1842, the railroad came to Huntington as part of the mainline crossing from Farmingdale to Brentwood. The North Shore Line came into Huntington in 1867 and stopped at Northport, which was its terminus for six years. In 1873, this line was continued to Port Jefferson. The Long Island Rail Road (LIRR) main line was built as the faster means of transportation between New York and Boston by connecting with steamboat service at Greenport. (Ron Ziel Collection/ Huntington Historical Society.)

In 1867, when passengers arrived at the Huntington Railroad Station, there was nothing but open country north and south of the tracks. The original station house was built on grade on the north side of the tracks and west of New York Avenue, as seen in this early 1900s photograph. (Huntington Historical Society.)

Between 1909 and 1910, New York Avenue was bridged by the Long Island Rail Road and became an underpass. A new depot was built, also on the north side of the tracks but this time on the east side of New York Avenue, where it stands today. Note the trolley tracks in the foreground and the two trolleys dropping off passengers by the railroad depot. (Huntington Historical Society.)

This 1915 view of the south side of the Huntington Depot shows the east, west, and cross-over tracks. As the train pulled into the station, the trainman would often throw shovelfuls of coal on the ground to be picked up by children and used to heat their homes. (Huntington Historical Society.)

This current-day photograph of the Huntington depot shows that the original building has not changed structurally. Differences include the raised platform and the electrified third rail. The four-tiered structure in the background is the newly constructed commuter parking garage. (Sforza collection.)

Railroad Station, Huntington, N. Y.

This is the north side of the Huntington Depot in the early 1900s. Note the interesting modes of transportation at the time—some people walking, the horse and buggy, a few automobiles, the trolley, and the Long Island Rail Road. In the early 1900s, walking was the primary means to get from place to place. (Huntington Historical Society.)

This is the Huntington depot as viewed from the north side today. There are not many people walking and a lot more automobiles. (Sforza collection.)

In 1901, the Thompson Book Company and the LIRR formed the Northport Traction Company. Trolley service began in Northport in 1902, first traveling from Woodbine Avenue to the Northport Railroad for a fee of 5¢ one way. Later, tracks were also laid on Main Street. Trolley service in Northport ceased in April 1924. The tracks can still be seen on Main Street. (Northport Historical Society.)

Notes written on the back of this photograph read, "Summer 1914. Left G. Henneborn, conductor, W. Whalters, mgr-adams exp., Henry Wehr, clerk, "Red" Bowden, driver, John Cook, motorman, Hennig, clerk, Oscar Fox, cow catcher." (Sforza Collection.)

In this image of the Halesite trolley turnabout, trolley cars and the new buses are waiting for the return trip to the Huntington Depot. With the proposed change from the trolley to gas-operated motor buses, transportation would not be limited to traveling north and south but would extend to also travel east and west. The gas-operated buses guaranteed the demise of the trolley system. (Huntington Historical Society.)

Years after the trolley service was discontinued, the trolley tracks were still visible despite the attempt to cover over them with blacktop. In this photograph, new-style buses continue mass transit during urban renewal in the 1960s. (Huntington Historical Society.)

Before the hard-surfaced roads of today, dirt roads were dusty on dry days and muddy on wet ones. Both conditions made travel difficult. This view of Irwin Place (on the west side of the present-day town hall) during mud season visually explains travel difficulty. (Huntington Historical Society.)

This image shows traffic on Main Street in the 1930s. Traffic congestion was exaggerated due to the fact that cars were not only allowed to curb park, but were also allowed to park down the middle of Main Street. (Huntington Historical Society.)

This is what Main Street traffic looks like today. (Sforza photograph.)

Henry Hanzik stands alongside his Cantrell Dodge wooden station wagon. In 1905, J.T. Cantrell Company started business in carriage building and repair in a three-story structure on Main Street. With the advent of the automobile, Cantrell changed his business to building bodies for cars. In 1915, Cantrell built a forerunner of the station wagon on a Model T chassis called a "depot wagon." By the 1920s, the J.T. Cantrell Company was building wooden bodies on all makes of automobiles. (Sforza photograph.)

In 1857, the Lloyd Harbor Lighthouse was built on a sand spit. The two-story, wood-framed dwelling had a brick foundation and a square, brick tower at one corner. There were three bedrooms on the top floor and a kitchen, dining room, and sitting room on the first floor. The original beacon was a fifth-order Fresnel lens that showed a fixed white light at a focal plane of 48 feet. (Huntington Historical Society.)

On August 11, 1857, Abiatha Johnson was appointed first keeper of the Lloyd Harbor Lighthouse. After Johnson's death, Robert McGlone assumed the title of keeper in 1886. The lighthouse was turned over to the state in 1926 and to the town of Huntington in 1928. The structure remained vacant until it was damaged by vandals and then destroyed by fire on November 12, 1947. (Huntington Historical Society.)

Seven

THE DAINTY AND
THE RICH

The Glenada Hotel in Cold Spring Harbor accommodated 600 guests. In early 1900s, it came into the possession of Walter Jennings, son-in-law of William Rockefeller, who had the hotel torn down to avoid having guests stroll in through the gates of his estate and admire his rare flowers. The casino, part of the Glenada, was gifted to the town, provided that it be moved to the other side of the village. (Town Clerk's Archives.)

Laurelton Hall was a large wood-frame summer hotel built by Dr. Oliver Jones on the west shore of Cold Spring Harbor near the Glenada and Forest Lawn Hotels. The village of Laurel Hollow took its name from this hotel. At the turn of the 20th century, Louis Comfort Tiffany acquired the property, demolished the hotel, and built his famous mansion on the site. (Huntington Historical Society.)

By the early 1900s, the farm owned by George Biggs was located north of the depot, midway between Church and School Streets. Biggs built a hotel known as the North Side Hotel on the south end of his land, just north of the railroad station. The last owners were the Mullen family, who changed the name to Mullen's Hotel. In the mid-1930s, the hotel was demolished. (Huntington Historical Society.)

The Suffolk Hotel was one of the three major social centers in the town and was the terminal for Huntington stagecoaches. Patrons would assemble on its porch to watch the passing traffic. It was situated on the southwest corner of Main Street and New York Avenue. (Huntington Historical Society.)

Established in 1927 on the west end of Spring Lake in Centerport, Linck's Log Cabin was popular with the younger people. It went out of business in 1943 but later reopened. While waiting for food, one could play Match the Crockery, a challenging game since only a few pieces of the same pattern could be found. Today, the property is home to a group of condominiums called Courtyard Circle. (Greenlawn Centerport Historical Association.)

The National House Hotel was situated on the west side of New York Avenue, one block off Main Street. It was owned by William Fagan, who also owned the livery store next door. Next to the stables was Jackson's Blacksmith's Shop. (Huntington Historical Society.)

Located at Halesite, near the Abrams shipyard, was a summer resort named Edgewater Hotel, which was run by the Selleck family. (American Photograph Company, 1909.)

At the northeast corner of New York Avenue and Fairview Road stood the house and barn of Reuben S. Scudder, represented here around 1865. (Huntington Historical Society.)

Hotel Huntington opened its doors in 1929, replacing the house and barn of Reuben S. Scudder. Later, it was occupied by Oppenheim Collins, Franklin Simon, Millicent Kalt, and then Woolley's. In 1984, it became Aboff's Paint Store. The building was demolished in 2012 to be replaced by the TD Bank headquarters. (Huntington Historical Society.)

The Huntington Crescent Club began in the 1880s as the Crescent Athletic Club of Brooklyn, starting with rowing teams, polo fields, and the finest golf course. Today, it is one of the most prestigious clubs in Huntington, offering 6,403 yards of golf for a par of 70. The course was designed by Devereux Emmet and Alfred H. Tull of the American Society of Golf Course Architects and opened in 1931. (Huntington Crescent Club photograph.)

Otto Hermann Kahn built OHEKA Castle on a 443-acre plot at the highest point on Long Island, in Cold Spring Harbour. OHEKA, a five-story chateau patterned after the castles of France, was designed by William A. Delano. Olmstead Brothers, the firm founded by Central Park designer Frederick Law Olmstead, planned the bridle paths and gardens. Today, OHEKA is the second-largest private residence ever built in America. (Huntington Historical Society.)

The Chalmers House was the most popular hotel in Centerport. It started as a farmhouse, and towers were added in 1879 and 1888. The Order of Franciscan Brothers purchased property in Centerport, including the hotel, and built Mount Alvernia, the oldest Catholic summer camp in the nation. The building was demolished in 1980. (Greenlawn Centerport Historical Association.)

William K. Vanderbilt II was the great-grandson of railroad tycoon "Commodore" Cornelius Vanderbilt. The Vanderbilt mansion named Eagle's Nest, built in 1910, overlooks the Long Island Sound in Centerport. With his passion for automobiles, he built his own private, limited-access highway across much of Long Island and then instituted a series of popular car races. Today, the estate is a museum and planetarium. (Mattheou photograph.)

West Neck Farm is a 40-room, 30,000-square-foot mansion, designed in 1912 by architect Clarence Luce in the style of medieval French château for pharmaceutical magnate George McKesson Brown, who lost ownership after the 1929 stock market crash. The Brothers of the Sacred Heart acquired the property and named it Coindre Hall in memory of Father André Coindre, their founder. (Mattheou photograph.)

Born in Hamburg, Germany, August Heckscher immigrated to the United States in 1867. In 1918, Heckscher purchased the Prime property in Huntington and turned it into a park. Months later, in 1919, he erected a beautiful Beaux-Arts fine arts building, now the Heckscher Museum of Art. He and his wife were benefactors of the Soldiers & Sailors Memorial, the Huntington Hospital, and St. John's Episcopal Church. (Huntington Historical Society.)

Marshall Field III was an American investment banker and heir to the Marshall Field department store fortune. The department store, based in Chicago, grew to become a major chain before being acquired by Macy's in 2005. In 1920, Marshall Field III commissioned architect John Russell Pope to construct an English-style mansion on Long Island's North Shore, at Lloyd Neck. Today, the estate is preserved as Caumsett State Historic Park. (Mattheou photograph.)

Built in 1911 on 132 acres in Huntington Bay, the Monastery was designed as the summer home of Dr. Farquhar and Juliana Armour Ferguson. Although Farquhar Ferguson died before construction began, Juliana completed the couple's dream house. The gate house, still existing on East Shore Road, was modeled after a 17th-century Spanish carriage house and provided the entrance to the original estate. (Huntington Historical Society.)

The Bellas Hess estate, known as the Cedars, eventually encompassed about 150 acres and bordered New York Avenue, Oakwood Road, and McKay Road. Today, it is part of the Big H Shopping Center and Huntington High School. "Originally, there was a white farm house built on the highest portion of property. We could see the sailboats in the harbor," said June Hess Kelly. (Sforza collection/Hess collection.)

June Hess Kelly, daughter of Harry and Mabel Hess, was originally named Katherine Lorraine after her mother's best friends. When a friend mistakenly remarked how nice it was that her parents had called her June after the month in which she was born, she adopted June as her name. (Sforza collection/Hess collection.)

He Painted Ol' Man River

Born in New York City in 1815, John Banvard is famous for creating the largest painting in the world—a panorama of the Mississippi River. Measuring three miles long, it showed in detail the entire shore from the mouth of the Mississippi to the Gulf of Mexico. Banvard settled in Cold Spring Harbor at his house, which he named Glenada. (*New York Magazine*/town clerk's archives.)

Construction of the Roland Conklin house began in 1908. The design by architect Wilson Eyre (1858–1944), with its double gables and overhanging bays, is suggestive of old English manor houses. The formal gardens completed the design. The open-air amphitheater was built in 1918, and a curtain effect was created by the use of steam. A terraced area built into the hillside accommodated the audience. The estate encompasses 159 acres and is now incorporated into the St. Patrick's Seminary property. (Sforza collection/Hess collection.)

HALL'S FAMOUS SHORE DINNER
$2.50 Per Person

OLIVES   CLAM CHOWDER   RADISHES

STEAMED   CLAMS-BROTH

FISH   IN SEASON

COLD   LIVE
BOILED   BROILED

SPRING
BROILERS   MIXED SALAD

LONG ISLAND   IN
CORN   SEASON

MELON   ICE
CREAM

CHEESE   COFFEE

A la Carte

CIGARS
CIGARETTES

HALL'S ••• Centerport, L. I.
OPEN ALL YEAR
TELEPHONE NORTHPORT 90

Archie Hall's Chop House on Route 25-A and the southwest corner of Centershore Road opened in 1906 and became a popular driving destination. Teddy Roosevelt would often come from his house in Oyster Bay to dine at Hall's. (Greenlawn Centerport Historical Association.)

Geide's Hotel, which replaced Hall's, burned down in the 1960s. Later, a Howard Johnson's restaurant opened on this site, which would be replaced by Raynor's Chicken Restaurant in the 1980s. This is the present site of the Centerport Post Office. (Greenlawn Centerport Historical Association.)

Eight

FAMOUS PEOPLE

On September 8, 1776, Nathan Hale volunteered to go behind enemy lines and report on the movements of the British troops on Long Island. On September 21, he was arrested and brought for questioning before British commander Gen. William Howe. Hale was hanged on September 22 at the age of 21. He was the first American to be executed for spying on behalf of his country. (Sforza collection/Chase Bank collection.)

Son of Walter Whitman and Louisa VanVelsor, Walt Whitman was born in his father's farmhouse in West Hills in 1819. When 16 or 17, he taught in the schools of Long Island, and in 1838 he published the *Long Islander*. Published weekly to this day, the newspaper serves as the voice of the community. While working on the *Brooklyn Eagle*, Whitman published *Leaves of Grass* in 1855. (Walt Whitman Birthplace Association.)

Booker Taliaferro Washington was born into slavery in Virginia in 1856, the son of a slave woman and a white man from a neighboring farm. He learned to read and write and, at the age of 16, entered Hampton Institute to train as a teacher. In 1881, he founded the Tuskegee Institute, a vocational school in Tuskegee, Alabama. His summer home still stands in Fort Salonga, overlooking the Long Island Sound. (Thelma Jackson Abidally photograph.)

Silas Wood (1769–1847) served as the first historian of Long Island. He published the *History of Long Island* in 1824. He also served as state assemblyman and congressman for five terms. Wood lived for a time in a house on Park Avenue. (Huntington Historical Society.)

Hon. Henry L. Stimson was secretary of war under Pres. Franklin D. Roosevelt from 1940 to 1945. He fought as a combat officer in World War I; served in the cabinets of Presidents Taft, Hoover, and Franklin D. Roosevelt; and was a recipient of the Distinguished Service Medal. He made Huntington his home, and his family started what came to be known as the Annual Highhold Games. (Library of Congress.)

James Dewey Watson, a molecular biologist, geneticist, and zoologist, is best known as the co-discoverer of the structure of DNA with Francis Crick. Watson, Crick, and Maurice Wilkins were awarded the 1962 Nobel Prize in Physiology or Medicine for their discoveries concerning the molecular structure of nucleic acids and its significance for information transfer in living material. Watson has served the Cold Spring Harbor Laboratory since 1968 as its director, president, chancellor, and (currently) chancellor emeritus. (Watson Archives.)

Adm. Hiram Paulding (1797–1878) was a rear admiral in the US Navy. He purchased a farm of a few hundred acres in Lloyd Harbor from Samuel Bradhurst and, with his wife and daughter, established his home in 1837. The original house was a frame building with a wing on one end. Later, another wing was added, giving room for a family of six children. (Huntington Historical Society.)

Henry Fonda was an American film and stage actor and patriarch of the Fonda family of actors. After World War II, he docked his sailboat in Huntington Harbor for several summers and used to get his groceries from Joseph Costa's Main Street Fruit & Vegetable Market. (Sforza collection.)

Pat LaFontaine is a Hall of Fame hockey player who retired as one of the highest-scoring American-born players in NHL history. He married a girl from Huntington (Marybeth Hoey), and they have raised their three children in Lloyd Harbor. Active in many local charities, the LaFontaines started the Companions in Courage Foundation (www. CiC16.org), building interactive game rooms in children's hospitals across North America, including Huntington Hospital. (Jimmy Johnson/Pat LaFontaine.)

George Washington Brush was born in West Hills in 1842. While second lieutenant of the 34th US Colored Troops Company B, he was awarded the Medal of Honor in 1897. After his discharge from the military, he returned home and studied medicine, becoming one of the leading physicians of Kings County. He died in his home, the Hotel Chatelin in Brooklyn, in 1927. (Huntington Historical Society.)

Billy J. Kramer (née William Howard Ashton) grew up in Liverpool, England. The first in his succession of popular smash hits in the 1960s was written for him by John Lennon and Paul McCartney. This song claimed the No. 1 spot in England, toppling the Beatles themselves. Among his international million-sellers was his worldwide hit "Little Children." Billy and his wife, Roni, lived in Huntington for 16 years. (Billy J. Kramer photograph.)

The Lockhorns is a single-panel comic created in 1968 by Bill Hoest. Distributed worldwide by King Features Syndicate, it appears in 500 newspapers in 23 countries. Bill Hoest died in 1988, but his widow, Bunny Hoest, continues the strip with Bill's longtime assistant, John Reiner. Both Bunny and John are longtime Huntington residents. (Both, Bunny Hoest.)

THE LOCKHORNS

"READY?"

Edith Storey (1892–1967) was a silent film star of the Vitagraph Company. She appeared in *Dust of Egypt, Eyes of the Mystery, The Christian, Susie the Sleuth* and many westerns. She retired in Asharoken and served as the clerk of the Incorporated Village of Asharoken from 1932 to 1960. During World War II, her home became the drop-off point for materials collected for the war effort. Edith spent the final years of her life in an apartment on Main Street in Northport. (Northport Historical Society.)

Don Grolnick may best be known for the 22 years he collaborated with James Taylor as his keyboard player and musical director. But he also was a brilliant jazz composer, recording several albums under his own name. Don performed with the best of his generation—including Linda Ronstadt, Steely Dan, and Michael Brecker. His parents resided in East Northport, and they served as inspiration until he passed from non-Hodgkins lymphoma in 1996, at age 48. (Mrs. Don Grolnick and Jimmy Johnson.)

Composer and pianist Sergei Rachmaninoff, known for his work "Symphonic Dances," rented the Honeyman Estate near Northport Harbor with his wife, Natalia. The Rachmaninoffs stayed here from 1940 until they bought a house in California in 1942. The decision to live in Northport was based on the fact that Sergei's first cousin, Dr. Sophie Satina, was working on chromosome research at Cold Spring Harbor Laboratory from 1923 to 1943. (Greenlawn Centerport Historical Association.)

Taken on the occasion of Fred Sforza's 77th year in his Huntington shoe repair business, this photograph shows, from left to right, Assemblyman Andrew Raia, Assemblyman James D. Conte, Fred Sforza, and Huntington Town Clerk Jo-Ann Raia, longest-serving town clerk, responsible for the establishment of the town's archives. Conte, a lifelong resident of Huntington Station, was first elected to the New York State Assembly on March 15, 1988. Throughout his career, he always maintained a strong sense of community with Huntington Station and never forgot his roots. A 25-year veteran of the assembly, he died on October 16, 2012, at the age of 53. (Sforza collection.)

Lt. Gen. Frank Libutti is a Vietnam War veteran and the youngest Marine in history to achieve the rank of general. After retiring in 2001, he became the first New York City counterterrorism commissioner and later the undersecretary for information analysis and infrastructure protection for the Department of Homeland Security. A local street is named after him. (Jeannine Libutti.)

Seen in the front row of this image, taken on the front steps of Huntington High School, is Leroy Grumman (1895–1982) who was an aeronautical engineer, test pilot, and industrialist. He was born in Huntington and, from an early age, demonstrated an interest in aviation. In his June 20, 1911, salutatory address at Huntington High School, Grumman predicted that the final perfection of the aeroplane would be one of man's greatest triumphs over nature. In 1929, he cofounded Grumman Aeronautical Engineering Company. (Huntington High School collection.)

Alexander Gardiner was born in 1835. His estate, Gardiner's Lake, comprised 600 acres west of Greenlawn Village. During the 1860s, he built what was the largest cider mill on Long Island at one time. The pickle works on his property processed the pickles grown on the Gardiner farm and those grown on many neighboring farms. In 1864, his sawmill produced large amounts of oak and chestnut lumber to be sold to local boatbuilders. (Greenlawn Centerport Historical Association.)

Sgt. Elijah Churchill was awarded the first Purple Heart medal by Gen. George Washington. Elijah was wounded during the capture of Fort Slongo (now Fort Salonga) on October 3, 1781, while leading his troops into the fort. The fort was burned to the ground, and most of the British soldiers were captured. At present, there is a tavern bearing the name Elijah Churchill in Fort Salonga. (Northport Historical Society.)

In 1914, Cornelia Prime donated a house located on five acres of land on Park Avenue for a new hospital. The nine-bed Winkworth Cottage Hospital on New Street could no longer meet the needs of a growing community. The second building of Huntington Hospital opened in 1933, following a campaign for funds sponsored by the Huntington Chamber of Commerce. The original hospital still stands today, adjacent to the main structure. (Huntington Historical Society.)

In 1920, August Heckscher opened a museum and park for the benefit of the people of Huntington and the surrounding region. Operated by a private foundation, the museum presented works by old masters, such as Henry Raeburn, as well as American painters like Asher B. Durand. In 1954, the Town of Huntington took ownership of the institution. (Mattheou photograph.)

Nine

HUNTINGTON TODAY

During the 1950s, it became apparent that the old town hall building could no longer accommodate the town's government. In December 1974, a town hall task force reported that, including acquisition, refurbishing the building, road improvements, and parking facilities, the Huntington R.L. Simpson Jr. High School was the better choice for a new town hall. The former school has been the town hall since 1979. (Craig P. Wolff photograph.)

At the end of the 19th century, the Brooklyn Institute of Arts and Sciences founded a laboratory for training high school and college teachers in marine biology. In 1889, John D. Jones gave land and buildings, formerly part of the Cold Spring Whaling Company, to the institute. Courses at the new Biological Laboratory began in 1890, establishing education in the biological sciences as the Cold Spring Harbour Laboratory's first mission. (Mattheou photograph.)

Libutti Diamond Jewelers was established in 1943 by Mario Libutti, who started repairing watches in his mother's kitchen. Still occupying the original site, it continues to be run by family members and has tripled in size. It specializes in custom designs, expert gemologists and jewelers, appraisals, and extensive watch expertise. (Jeannine Libutti photograph.)

Founded in 1886, the Cold Spring Harbor Public Library serves the communities of Cold Spring Harbor, Laurel Hollow, and Lloyd Harbor. (Mattheou photograph.)

Established in 1759, the Huntington Public Library is one of the oldest public libraries in Suffolk County. Rev. Ebenezer Prime was the first "library-keeper." In 1892, the library association constructed the Soldiers & Sailors Memorial Building, which housed the new library. In July 1958, the library was moved to its present location, the former New York Telephone Company building. (Huntington Public Library/Wurts Brothers Photographers.)

The J.W. Engeman Theater at Northport was established in 2006 when Kevin and Patti O'Neill purchased the building of the old Northport Theater. They renamed it after Patti's brother, Chief Warrant Officer Four John William Engeman, who was killed in Iraq in 2006. The theater is Long Island's only year-round professional theater company, offering stadium-style seating, a full orchestra pit, and a classic wood-paneled piano lounge with full bar. (Mattheou photograph.)

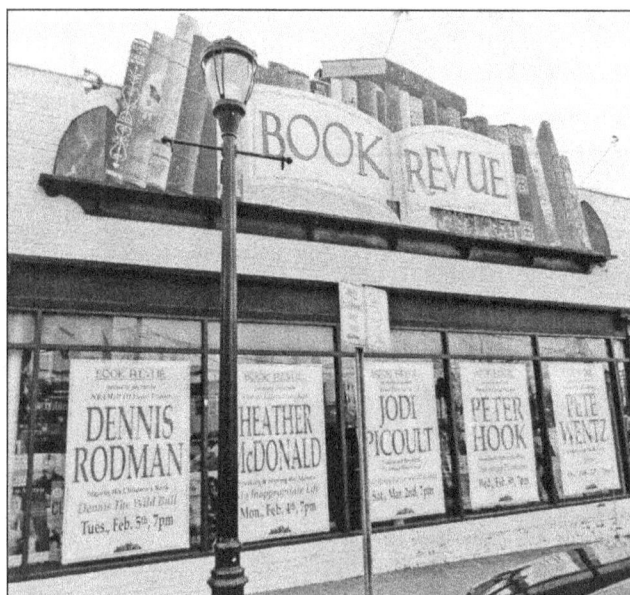

Book Revue has been a family-owned bookstore since 1977, selling new, used, rare, collectable, and discounted books. The store has expanded five times since it was founded. It is one of the largest independent bookstores in the country, providing quality bookselling to the Huntington community for many years. Authors who have appeared at Book Revue have included presidents; senators; astronauts; sports, television, and Hollywood stars; and many local and independent writers. (Mattheou photograph.)

The Cold Spring Harbour Whaling Museum opened in 1942. The museum's holdings of 6,000 artifacts document the whaling and maritime history of the region. Highlights of the collection include New York state's only fully equipped 19th-century whaleboat with original gear, a notable scrimshaw collection, and records of the Long Island Coastwise Trade Under Sail, and of the Cold Spring Harbour Customs House (1798–1908). (Mattheou photograph.)

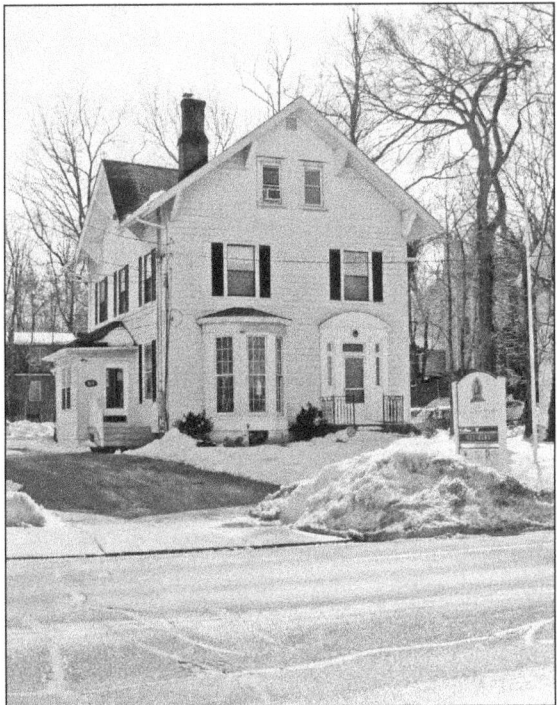

The Huntington Chamber of Commerce was founded in 1925. Its mission has been to promote industry and economic growth within the greater Huntington area. Among its greatest accomplishments have been the replacement of trolley cars with motor-bus service to Huntington Harbour from the Long Island Rail Road in 1927; the initiation and planning for the construction of Hotel Huntington in 1929; and the campaign for the opening of the second hospital building in 1933. (Mattheou photograph.)

Finnegan's Pub was established in 1912 on Wall Street by Andrew Finnegan Sr., who was once cited by Robert Ripley in *Ripley's Believe It or Not* as "the good bartender of Huntington, New York—45 years a bartender and never tasted liquor or smoked tobacco." This was the location of Huntington House, which was an important gathering place from 1816 on. (Mattheou photograph.)

Born in Brooklyn on July 13, 1913, Fred Sforza came to Huntington in 1934 to take over his brother-in-law's shoe-repair business. He is affectionately called "Freddie the shoemaker" and the "mayor of Huntington Station." For the next 79 years, Freddie's Shoe Repair serviced the Huntington community, creating a record that will be hard to beat. At 98 years of age, he still goes to his store four days a week. (Len Totora photograph.)

In 1914, the Ketewamoke Chapter of the Daughters of the American Revolution purchased this house for $2,500. The Ketewamoke Chapter took its name from the Native American word for the region around Huntington, and the term is believed to mean "the place having the best beach or shore." The house is in the National Register of Historic Places. The chapter remains active in diverse programs dealing with local and national activities. (Lillian Najarian/Huntington Historical Society.)

The Huntington Arts Council was founded in 1963 as a not-for-profit organization assisting art organizations and individual artists. Designated by the New York State Council on the Arts as "vital to the cultural life of New York State," it is also the official arts-coordinating agency for Huntington. It serves as the primary regranting agency on Long Island for the New York State Council on the Arts. (Mattheou photograph.)

Simon Hirschfeld's was the first Jewish family to settle in Huntington in 1872. He owned and operated a general store on the corner of Main and New Streets. His son Jacob opened a clothing store, the Toggery, before switching to real estate and insurance in the 1920s. Today, J.W. Hirschfeld Agency on Main Street is still owned and operated by the third generation of the Hirschfeld family. (Hirschfeld family photograph.)

In 1907, Congress appropriated $40,000 for construction of a new lighthouse at the entrance to both Lloyd Harbor and Huntington Harbor. The new structure, completed in 1912, was unique in both design and construction. The Venetian Renaissance style makes the lighthouse look like a small castle. The original lantern was a fifth-order Fresnel lens. The lighthouse structure remains the same today as in 1911. (Viewpoint photography/Pam Setchell.)

ABOUT THE HISTORICAL SOCIETY

The Huntington Historical Society was organized in 1903 as part of the celebration of the town's 250th anniversary (1653–1903). It is distinguished as one of the oldest repositories of local history in the New York metropolitan area, maintaining a collection of artifacts, a library, and archival holdings that document and preserve priceless relics of Huntington's rich past. In 1911, the society acquired the 1750 David Conklin House and has continued to maintain it as a museum for over 100 years. Today, the society owns four historic properties in and around the village of Huntington and manages seven historic structures, including the 1795 Daniel W. Kissam House, the 1892 Soldiers & Sailors Memorial Building, and the 1905 Trade School Building.

Through a combination of exhibitions, historic house tours, craft classes, genealogy workshops, seasonal festivals, special events, and public educational programs, the society uses its resources to provide services to diverse audiences. The society has the dual role of preserving a vast collection of artifacts of Huntington's founding families while also providing newcomers with a sense of place and identity in a town proud of its deep historical roots.

The collection of 18th-, 19th-, and 20th-century decorative arts are displayed in the two house museums and three galleries that are open to the public. The society's resource center and archive, located on two floors of the Trade School, is recognized as a regional research facility. It houses one of the area's most comprehensive photographic collections, with over a quarter million images spanning the entire period of photography and providing a valuable record of the central Long Island region. Plans are at hand for expanding the 209 Main Street building.

—Robert (Toby) Kissam
Executive Director of the Huntington Historical Society

Visit us at
arcadiapublishing.com